Peace & goodwill

Bill Bertrand

Wild Flowers

Longing for Belonging

William Bertrand and Cynthia Stork

◆ FriesenPress

One Printers Way
Altona, MB R0G0B0,
Canada

www.friesenpress.com

Copyright © 2021 by William Bertrand and Cynthia Stork

First Edition — 2021

Cover illustration by Serine Zaatout, twitter.com/SerineZaa

All rights reserved.

No part of this publication may be reproduced in any form, or by any means, electronic or mechanical, including photocopying, recording, or any information browsing, storage, or retrieval system, without permission in writing from FriesenPress.

ISBN
978-1-03-910607-9 (Hardcover)
978-1-03-910606-2 (Paperback)
978-1-03-910608-6 (eBook)

1. *Poetry*

Distributed to the trade by The Ingram Book Company

Other books by William Bertrand

LOVE SNACKS
Let's have a poetry party!!

Poetry by
WILLIAM BERTRAND
Illustrations by FRANCES ENRIQUEZ

Love Snacks: Let's have a poetry party!!

Table of Contents

Introduction i

Perfect Gift 1

Undiscovered Gift 3

Gift of Life and Light 5

Unwanted Gift 7

A Stitch in Time 9

Gift of Family 11

Gift of Giving and the Giving of the Gift 13

The Gift is not a Birthright 15

Exploited Gift 17

Gift in Disguise 19

Just in Time Gift 21

Gifted Personality 23

Gift of Renewal 25

A Day of Prayer 27

Ever Tall, Ever Small	29
A Rainbow of Friends is the Lord's Delight	31
Dancing Through the Raindrops	33
I love you; you love me	37
I love to be with you	39
Invitations	41
Gift of Belonging for the Wild Flowers	45
Roses and Sunshine	49
Amazing and Wonderful	51
Place your Hands in the Hands of Love	53
One day at a time, Alleluia	55
Be Young, be Innocent	57
Each Moment, I Cherish, Emmanuel	59
Concluding Remarks	61
Group Discussion Topics	63

For all the Wild Flowers
Longing for Belonging

And our wonderful caregivers
Who help us grow

Introduction

Cynthia and I met at a food-service mission in a Church in Esquimalt. We would go there for lunch and fellowship with other members. Cynthia and some of her friends were students at a University Humanities Program. When I met Cynthia through a common friend, she was a member of a social service club. Cynthia was an active member, recruiting new members, and volunteering to help clients sign up for benefits. Cynthia was also a licensed caregiver, and she helped to take care of a regular client and would help him in the hobby of writing songs. Well, it was not long before Cynthia invited me to join the club, which I did. We went to the club house and soon started to do some writing exercises. I came up with the idea to write about the various kinds of gifts. I added some material that I previously wrote to add more substance and to delve deeper into the gift of healing, then decided not to have illustrations but to add some songs instead. After showing the manuscript to Cynthia, she discovered that we both had a longing to belong. Thus, we titled our book, Wild Flowers: Longing for Belonging.

Cynthia and I differ in our creativity. Cynthia says, "I talk—talk faster than I think. Remembering I can never do. I work with my hands faster than I can remember what I do, because I am talking to myself and my subconscious instincts inter-self. Mind is good. No issues with performance or integrity of ingenuity." Cynthia thinks that, when she is talking with me, she would like me to record her on the computer. "This way, when you make a telephone call, you can generate ideas faster."

I can relate with this way of capturing ideas, because many times when I am creating a symphonic tune verbally, it comes out of me and vanishes into the air, and then I cannot remember it. When I am writing song lyrics, I've come into the habit of carrying paper and a pen in my shirt pocket. Often, I'll hear a short, whispered phrase, and then write it down. Then I sit down and intersperse my memories with these whispered phrases to come up with a poetic song. Then I come up with a tune while going out for a singing walk. "So, where do these whispered phrases come from?" you might ask. I tend to hold my emotions in, and then later, there is a breaking open and purging of these emotions, and the Holy Spirit then puts words to them. Another way the words come to me is through racing thoughts in the middle of the night. I have learned how to listen to these thoughts, acknowledge them, and let them fall like snowflakes from Heaven upon the mountaintop and into the valleys.

It is good to be able to listen, pay attention, and have a child-like wonder, not forgetting how to sing and play. Cynthia and I are both young at heart and friends with the Bible. We hope that you enjoy our poems and insight, and connect yourself with the source and love of the wonderful "Gift of Healing" to (as Cynthia says) "recapture the infinity of each day as we awaken to a new dawn that regenerates our belonging."

Group Discussion Topic

Moving to a new city

1. Why did you or would you re-locate?
2. What were/are your expectations?

Perfect Gift

By Cynthia Stork

I am for having the perfect gift:
    Sleep, being relaxed, and survival.

I am at the lake on the water,
    Talking, singing, and swimming.
    I feel like a fish with a wish list

    For the perfect gift.
Here I am, wiggling around,
    Dancing, chatting, wanting more of me,
    In self-expression of being the sun-dance queen.
The sun is hot, and I am on my water-bed,
    Tanning to a golden raisin brown.

From dawn to dusk, I hustle
    To do my best to get good movement
    In the water for my leisure time,
    To have three months non-stop for me,
Come what may, come what will.

Inspiration is from within seen,
    It's for you and me to share.
    This day and every day is flowing free,
Need not may, need not say.

The expressions are free;
    Power within, power withheld:
    This is the perfect gift in every way.

Undiscovered Gift

By William Bertrand

Vocation, vocation, vocation....
    What is my vocation?
If you want to join us,
    You need a university degree!
Let us pray for vocations:
    Mother Mary, let us be!
So, I chose service, service, and service,
    And with a bagged lunch, hospitality.
Who is that girl?
    I have to sit next to her!
Over and over again,
    I have met these people without looking.
Maybe we can meet sometime soon.
    Shall we go out for a milkshake?
All of the people who came my way,
    And we befriended each other:
    These were my undiscovered gifts
Revealed to me by strangers.

Group Discussion Topic

Being a stranger

1. How does it feel to be on the "Outside"?
2. How have knocking on doors, seeking opportunities, and asking for help been working out for you?
3. What do you have to offer in relationships?

Gift of Life and Light

By Cynthia Stork

Gift of life-light takes flight,
    In the right time of the night.

May might make it a night.
    By the moonlit night, and at noon,
    I soon will be drinking in sunlight.

The right cup of tea
    Or tea for two or tea just for me;
    Nine lives cat will chat with me.

His is of milk; my tea is light
    As I read the giver of life book.

The gift is the Bible; the tea is of friends:
    This is the tranquility reading of you and me.

The gift comes in time for life reading of the Bible;
    Shine on me life-light!

Group Discussion Topic

"Digging your well"- connecting to supports

1. What kind of supports do you need?
2. How do you connect to your supports?

Unwanted Gift

By William Bertrand

She was wrapped in a dress
    And popped up out of the birthday cake.
"Happy birthday," she said;
    Then everyone sang, "Happy birthday…"
    But nobody wanted her.
She felt used and rejected every time.
What a way to make a living!
She got paid for her personality

He was big and strong;
    A member of the football team,
    All of the cheerleaders adored him.
He was the master of ceremonies.
He knew how to entertain the audience.
He had the gift of the gab and humour.
I aspired to have these qualities, and when I received them,
    I was an unwanted gift for some and cherished by others.

Group Discussion Topic

Forging new paths

1. What kind of ventures have you tried to organize and implement?
2. How do you handle obstacles, rejection and failure?

A Stitch in Time

By Cynthia Stork

A cat has nine lives.
    So, what can I do to do a stitch in time?
Save it for a new stitch on my new patchwork,
    Or for a new gift for my new coat.
An interchangeable badge is used on many coats.
Sewing, playing cards, and drinking tea at the table.
    I did all of the linen myself.
Drinking tea is very pleasant:
    Stitch in time with love in it
    Within my heart, to give a try for more linen.
It takes two to belong;
    That is how I prefer to spend the afternoon.
So, I will read before I go to bed
    Looking for more ideas.
The more that I sleep, the more that I read,
    The more of the more that is all about me.

Group Discussion Topic

Being a servant

1. Describe your process of getting established.
2. How have people helped you?
3. What are the joys and difficulties of your work?
4. How do you "recharge your batteries"?

Gift of Family

By William Bertrand

I moved away from home
    Just after I graduated from grade twelve;
    Now it has been thirty-eight years.
    It is a long time to be away from home.
Some years I have not seen my family at all.
On average, I only see my family
    For fourteen days each year.
It seems to me that I have been orphaned:
    Deprived of my family.
I know lots of people who are orphaned.
When I visit a senior's facility,
    There are hardly any visitors.
Hundreds of single young adults at the shelters
    Have been orphaned too.
    I am surrounded by orphaned people!

So, when I go home, it is nice to be with family
    And the separation anxiety goes away.

Group Discussion Topic

Longing to go home

1. How do you keep in touch with your family?
2. In what ways do you cherish your family?
3. What are some of the signs to come back home?

Gift of Giving and the Giving of the Gift

By Cynthia Stork

The gift of giving and the giving of the gift
    Are many things in a game of cards.
When kings and queens played people for cards,
    It was fun to have their power of knowing
    Who belongs to whom.
There are fifty-two cards in the deck.
    So, it is divided into four groups:
    Hearts, diamonds, clubs, spades,
    And the game is played to make these interchangeable.
We did not play with people,
    But we played with paper.
Paper is like the trees;
    Trees are like the tree of life.
    Life wasting nature is most valuable:
    This is the object truth of life itself.
Life is for real, and how things operate and cooperate
    Is the understanding of gain.

The name of the game is to gain insight on the truth of the divine;

    The way of life is unchangeable "at hand."

The Gift is not a Birthright

By Cynthia Stork

It is not a birthright,
    Because it is not a right on paper
    To prove the order of life.
    The order of life has not been
    To enhance—to give order to the giver of life.
    Your life is going to be what you want,
    But the birth is only the beginning to the giver of life.

Time over time is a way to see the sun
    And know the son of life is the giver of life:
    This is light for everyone to see.

To use more water, and to water the land for man,
    This is to give back to the giver.

This is not a birthright,
    Because man has to give the right gift
    To write an order on paper:
    Every day is a rebirth not depending on words written on paper.

Group Discussion Topic

Renewal

1. What in life do you take for granted?
2. How have your attitudes changed over time?
3. How do you give back to our Creator?

Exploited Gift

By Cynthia Stork

The exploited gift is when,
    Giving someone a gift of giving,
    It is not received, because it is talk
    But no action, words of order on page.

Exploitation is talked about, but the information is not given
    Nor put into action with a gift well received because of the
    Unknown wanting of action.
    To have is to hold,
    To claim what is owned and really belong
    When it is all said and done.

Who is to say who is to do for, what it is worth
    In the weight of gold, or in the weight of the dust to
    Go with the wind?

The daylight is near; so is the dust stirring to return to the Earth.
Dear heart, don't stop stirring; time is still ringing.

Group Discussion Topic

Exploitation

1. In what ways are you being exploited and oppressed?
2. How does it feel to not be valued?
3. What parts of your life do you need to improve?

Gift in Disguise

By William Bertrand

In a city of expensive houses,
    Lack of affordable apartments and low wages,
    How do service people survive?
Thank God for community kitchens!
There are many volunteers serving
    And many organizations behind the scenes
    Supplying food and resources.
Prayers are said before each meal.
Thanksgiving is said when we are well fed.
For hope and encouragement
    We are schooled together in a community meal.
We make friends as we dine together.
This city could use more services like this.
You never know who you will meet.
Sometimes someone is a gift in disguise.
You can't tell by the clothes that they wear!

Group Discussion Topic

Welcoming a stranger

1. How welcoming are you to strangers?
2. Tell a story about discovering goodness in a stranger.

Just in Time Gift

By William Bertrand

Ever have a just in time gift?
Think of the health care that we have
    Available with just a phone call.
It is quite amazing if you think about it.
And if you do, not many can hold all of the knowledge
    Inside their head!
Just think of all the inventions over the past fifty years.
All of the study that health care employees undertake
    To become qualified caregivers.
Think of all of the money invested in infrastructure
    And all of the research and development.
A gift for all of society!
So for a person like me who has received such a gift
    It is a pleasure to be able to be there in small ways
    To lend a helping hand and be able to contribute
    With my free time.

Group Discussion Topic

Giving and receiving blessings

1. In what ways have people been blessing you?
2. How have you been a blessing to others?
3. Who in your life are you thankful for? Why?

Gifted Personality

By William Bertrand

What is a gifted personality?
Is it someone who gets all of the girls?
Is it someone who gets the best jobs?
And makes all of the money?
Some people are gifted with ingenuity
    But cannot relate with people.
Some people cannot change a lightbulb
    But can light up a room with their presence.
I was looking for my first job
    After I failed my first year of college.
Some neighbour said to me,
    "Why don't you apply to work at the hospital?"
So, I went to apply.
    I felt very intimidated by the application form.
I said to my aunt, "I have neither credentials nor experience."
She said to me, "You have big ears and a big smile!"

Group Discussion Topic

Gifts

1. What are your personal gifts?
2. How do you like to share your gifts?

Gift of Renewal

By Cynthia Stork and William Bertrand

Being made brand new again.
    In ways that the eyes could not understand.
The receiving from the light of knowing, it
    Can begin again to give a renewal gift a chance.

My second kindergarten:
    Getting to know my classmates with trust.
    Toss the ball, catch the ball,
    Say your name, remember their name.
We played music with
    Drums, tambourines, shakers, and piano.
Words, stories, sharing…. Where do you come from?
    No prying, please, too sensitive.
Feelings, more feelings, letting go.
Graduations, more school, more graduation:
    Regeneration.

The people gather to give renewal of their ideas.
Beginning to see for their thinking
    That the old stories still have meaning:

    Learning to share, no matter who you are,
    Or where you come from.

The gift to bring people together
    Was of them knowing
    What the light of the Lord meant,
    And the sun is the biggest star by day,
    And the moon by light night.

I came for healing
    And people came to help.

This works nicely with the outer stars of the night;
    Daylight starlight,
    The wish of the perfect gift of renewal
For the world to enjoy.

A Day of Prayer
By William Bertrand

Drop on by for a day of prayer
Rest for a while in an easy chair
My love is quite a good listener
Qualities a disciple would have

She taps a tune with the palm of her hand
Could she be sending me a message?
I sing to her a nursery rhyme
Can we really be so childish?

Cross on over to restful valley
Peaceful summers, quiet winters
Where the aged live and ponder
Would you like to join them too?

She who traveled the road before you
She who married love that passed away
She who waits for some affection
Will you be affection for her?
I could possibly work myself away
There is only so much of me to go around

William Bertrand and Cynthia Stork

In meeting friend after friend
With open windows to heaven

Hear your heart in the neighbour beside you
Bring your friends; what a possibility
The meadow glorious and in full bloom
Seeds of love for eternity

Ever Tall, Ever Small

By William Bertrand

How about a dance tonight?
It has been so long
It has been so long
You came crying from a lonely shore
Wouldn't it be nice
To share some time together?

Let's go out to explore
I'll show you a different life
Hold my hand
Hold my hand
I will show you to understand
What love is meant to be

Ever tall, ever small
Love is meant for one and all
All us tired and lonely people
Love is meant for one and all

How about some brand-new friends?
Our friendship seemed to drift apart

William Bertrand and Cynthia Stork

In all our work
We neglect each other
We need some rain to satisfy
The thirst of our tender roots

Can you afford some time alone?
Love will meet you there
I will meet you in the quiet
I will meet you in the splendour of creation
With you never apart

Ever tall, ever small
Love is meant for one and all
All us tired and lonely people
Love is meant for one and all

A Rainbow of Friends is the Lord's Delight

By William Bertrand

A rainbow of friends
Is the Lord's delight
With love passed on
From generation to generation
A rainbow of friends
Is the Lord's delight
A wonderful sight for the world to see
The bow extends from east to west
With hope for God's goodness for rich and poor
The bow extends from east to west
A love invitation for humanity
God ever present
God ever loving
O when your people practice living their faith
Their good deeds shine throughout the world

Thank you for being a faithful friend

Group Discussion Topic

Diversity

1. How broad and diverse are your friendships?
2. How do you practice your faith?

Dancing Through the Raindrops

By William Bertrand

Clouds pour out their wanted rain
Dancing through the raindrops
Freshness to renew my brain
Dancing through the raindrops
Come renew my life again
Purge the sadness that's within
Transform all my energy
Dancing through the raindrops

Wonder water from above
Rain on us, Heaven's love
Trees rejoice, flowers bloom
Come outside from your room
Rainbow shining in the sky
Birds sing out as you walk by
Makes you want to sing along
Dancing through the raindrops

Time to visit some new friends
Dancing through the raindrops
Learning how to circulate
Dancing though the raindrops
Like a mountain stream and lake
Come into community
Meeting new friends sure feels great
Dancing though the raindrops

Want new life? Zest and fire?
Is that what you desire?
New purpose and uplifting
Get up and dance and sing with me!

Reach across the distant shore
For new possibility
To someone else's door
It's within your ability
Be a guest; then be a friend
Come together in the end
Let's join hands and celebrate
Dancing through the raindrops
Clouds pour out their wanted rain
Dancing through the raindrops
Freshness to renew my brain
Dancing though the raindrops
Come renew my life again
Purge the sadness that's within

Transform all my energy
Dancing through the raindrops

Rainbow shining in the sky
Birds sing out as you walk by
Makes you want to sing along
Dancing through the raindrops
Rainbow shining in the sky
Birds sing out as you walk by
Makes you want to sing along
Dancing though the raindrops

Group Discussion Topic

Tears of Joy

1. Describe a situation when you had tears of joy when you were liberated?
2. How does it feel to be refreshed?
3. In what new ways are you moving forward?

I love you; you love me

By William Bertrand

I love you; you love me
We are going to find you a family
Because I love you

You dance with me; I dance with you
Sometimes I go and step on your shoe
But you know that I still love you

Thoughts of marriage in my head
Tossing and turning in my bed
I know you are waiting for me

I see you on the street now and then
You are so shy; we can be friends
Because I know that God does love you

When poverty comes to your front door
Sooner or later, you will want more
Pass the cookies please
Come with me, and I will show you
A rainbow life of love

William Bertrand and Cynthia Stork

Sitting there all alone
Waiting for a friend to find a home

I think of love, and I think of you
All alone on a rainy night
Nowhere to rest your head
And you found me through a friend

Come share some time
We can be friends

I love to be with you

By William Bertrand

In the morning when I say my prayers
I'm with you; I love to be with you
In the morning when I say my prayers
I'm with you; I love to be with you

I count my blessings with my two hands
And then I give them back to you
I count my blessings with my two hands
And then I give them back to you

All day we laugh and play
All day we learn your ways
Each day you show to us
What love is really, really all about
What love is really, really all about

I like to court you with the earth and sky
Because I want to marry you
I like to court you with the earth and sky
Because I want to marry you

For what could be better
Than making my girlfriend
Happy in my thanksgiving?
Would you like to have a piece
Of home-made apple pie?

All day we laugh and play
All day we learn your ways
Each day you show to us
What love is really, really all about
What love is really, really all about

Catch a smile with the rising sun
Share your joy with the lonely ones
You break bread so easily
Live your life with simplicity

Hear the rain from the window sill
Hear the voice of our Father's will
Rejuvenate your tired soul
Bathe in silence to make you whole

All day we laugh and play
All day we learn your ways
Each day you show to us
What love is really, really all about
What love is really, really all about

Invitations

It is hard to describe the amount of learning and growth that I experienced with my illness during the last thirty years. I cannot talk like a doctor, a nurse, or a priest, although I have received much help from these groups of people. So I will talk as a struggling survivor. There is so much thanksgiving in my healing that has resulted in my returning thanks by volunteering in the community. I must begin by saying "Thank you for your invitation."

Society is full of people who are inviting others to share and enjoy life. I can think of the hockey teams that I played on with the coaches and trainers and all of the people working behind the scenes to make the hockey league happen. My parents gave me my high school year book. Looking through the pages were pictures of us students having lots of fun with all sorts of activities, all supported by our teachers. I can remember being invited to weddings of family and friends celebrating new life and new beginnings.

When I was sick and in care, our care givers organized all sorts of outings, nature walks, and parties to nurse us patients back into good health. When I was feeling better, with the help of a work program, I applied for work, I received an invitation for an interview, and then I was offered a job. I became a member of a work team. Thank you so much for all of these invitations.

After accepting these various invitations I became part of a group. At my work place I became a helper. I was trained to do various tasks that were part of my job. My self-confidence started to grow and so did my communication skills. I started to reach out to expand my life by knocking on more doors to see if I could join more activities. I went back to school. Intellectual study and group projects helped my brain to think in new ways and to strengthen my brain. And by going to church I was able to cry and receive healing for my heart. Inside these groups was where I met friends. There sure are a lot of blessings with friendship and that is another story. Basically, I was learning from people more so than from books. And I learned that people and systems worked together, collaborated together, and are coordinated together. I learned that the big field is made up of a lot of smaller fields each interconnected. I had relatively small tasks to do in my contributions.

While I was volunteering, I noticed that there was a big need for helping assistance from society and I took it to heart to try to fill the need. Poor me with my small heart, I was like a small heater trying to heat the outside winter cold. Too much heart work made me realize that I have to start working in my small part of the field, work with my hands, and sing and play again. Working too much in the big field consumed too much of me and I neglected some of my close friends. For this I need forgiveness.

So, after being invited to join groups, I participated, I learned, I contributed, I enjoyed, then I in turn became a person to invite friends to share in the goodness that I received, thus, multiplying grace. I hope that you find happiness and joy with caring, sharing, and helping one another knowing that small communions make up the whole of our community. Let's try to take care of our loved ones the best we can so as not to get isolated, longing for the day when the pandemic is over and we can celebrate life again as a human family.

Group Discussion Topic

Becoming a good friend

1. Describe the process of becoming a friend.
2. What kinds of activities do you like to participate in?
3. Why is friendship important to you?
4. Describe your home away from home and extended family.

Gift of Belonging for the Wild Flowers

By William Bertrand

Some people with mental illness, like me, are like the wild flowers that Jesus talks about in the Bible. When a person with mental illness is brought into care for cultivation, their job is to work with their caregivers. With the help of the caregiver, people with mental illness have their work to do. I had to learn how to work with my emotional labour. I had to work socially to develop friendships. I had to learn communication skills. I had to learn how to listen. I had to learn how to reason. I had to learn and practice to put words to my emotions. I had to learn how to self-regulate and manage my behaviour. I had to learn how to work through the grieving process. I had to learn how to forgive. I had to learn how to see and hear the world and other people with new eyes and ears. I needed to see colour instead of black and white—beauty instead of grey. I needed to learn how to trust. I needed to come to acceptance. Wow! This was quite the learning and growing journey that I was on!

This happened one day at a time with joy and sorrow, challenges and fun, and with prayers for mercy not to be too overwhelmed. Thank you for all of the support!

So, what is the vocation of the "wild flower" like me? It is to receive God, sing God's praise, and befriend. There are many people who have made it their life-long vocation to befriend "wild flowers" and support them, and in the process, they too have become God's friends. A "wild flower's" vocation may change as they mature and grow in God's goodness. They may support other "wild flowers". They may help the isolated people to unite into community. They may also be able to help "strong trees" in their moments of weakness. I think that it is important for the cultivated church to get to know the "wild flowers" in their community. "Wild flowers" need to be sought out and welcomed. What they really need is acceptance and can receive much help from a family of love and from a family of friends. This is the Great Discovery: knowing that we belong through the gift of friendship.

Dear Father of Love, please continue to bless and be present within all of us "wild flowers" for we are your little flock, and we welcome you into our hearts.

Dear Readers, for private reflection, prayerfully ponder the blessings you have received from the "wild flowers" in your life. How can you invite and engage in communion with the people who are on the fringes of your life: those who are newly discovered, and those who are forgotten or neglected? In what creative ways can you take care of the garden of your heart? Where can you meet new flowers; that is, new friends and blossom into a friend?

Group Discussion Topic

The makings of a great community

1. What are the features that make a great community?
2. What are the needs of your community?
3. How has your city helped you to grow?
4. In what ways can you become an inviting person?

Roses and Sunshine

By William Bertrand

Roses and sunshine
Rise up from your bed
Wake up little sparrows
It's almost breakfast time
Wake up, wake up
It's time to meet new friends
Wake up, wake up
The journey never ends

Father in Heaven
Loves little children
Jesus our brother
Bless little boys and girls
Wake up, wake up
It's time to meet new friends
Wake up, wake up
The journey never ends

Roses and tulips
Daffodils and daisies

William Bertrand and Cynthia Stork

You are my people
My treasure and joy
Pray to our Father
Be safe for a new day
Help out at church
Listen to God's voice

Wake up, wake up
It's time to meet new friends
Wake up, wake up
The journey never ends

All day long you watch over me
Never once did you scold me
Tenderly you do nourish me
You are a very good mother

Amazing and Wonderful
By William Bertrand

Isn't it amazing and wonderful
How two people meet again and again
Without looking for each other?

Isn't it amazing and wonderful
How two people meet again and again
Without looking for each other?
Looking for, looking for
Looking for each other

Until maybe one wishes and seeks her out
In foreign places and patterns of moving
Hoping and wondering if she feels the same?
Then the doors open; we're welcomed in
And the celebrations begin!

Isn't it amazing and wonderful
The power of the word "Hi" and a baby's cry?
When one starts and the others follow
Like a chain reaction, a communal baptism
Young and old both for the first time?

William Bertrand and Cynthia Stork

When we learn to worship in spirit and truth
In the presence of strangers
And God makes himself known

Isn't it amazing and wonderful?
Isn't it amazing and wonderful?
Isn't it totally amazing and wonderful!?

Place your Hands in the Hands of Love

By William Bertrand

Place your hands in the hands of love
And walk with us throughout this world
You do not have to travel far
To experience love of many kinds
Learn the words of a new love song
That is sung in tune by the gathering of children

Cultivate your love together
Marinate your soul with sounds
Of nature, nurturing a busy world
That is too tired to pray

Prayerful conversation, friend
Will surely bless all who dare to
Separate from the daily grind
Of the politics of noisy mass confusion

Come share with me some peaceful silence
Your faith, my faith, with God in between

William Bertrand and Cynthia Stork

This is one of the many ways
To let the kingdom come

A mighty roar!
The assembly is stirred!
Awaken love that lies sleeping
Look at the school
The children play!
This incarnation reappears
And rejuvenates the land

Let love take you out to the desert
And win you back with kindness and truth
When I feel that I am rejected
I welcome, welcome, Father's love

One day at a time, Alleluia

By William Bertrand

I am back to work with my doctor's note
Hear the song that I just wrote
Feel the beat of the tambourine
Keep in time with me

It is quite amazing what they can do
With a lab test and a scan or two
Take it out with a surgery
Take it one day at a time

One day at a time
One day at a time
One day at a time, alleluia
One day at a time

The sanctuary is the place to be
To get away from reality
From the people who won't let me be
So flourishing

Dreaming, planning, organizing
Overwhelming thoughts are rising
Business plans, rejection letters
Feeling mad in stormy weather

One day at a time
One day at a time
One day at a time, alleluia
One day at a time

Hanging out with my friends
I wish this day would never end
Sands of time in the hourglass
Take it one day at a time

Nature is a friend of mine
Where the river flows, she is kind
Bless the healthcare community
Take it one day at a time

One day at a time
One day at a time
One day at a time, alleluia
One day at a time

Be Young, be Innocent

By William Bertrand

I used to play cops and robbers
I used to play Superman
I used to play-fight with my father
And run just as fast as I can
With a tub of crayons
We coloured our books
More perfect throughout the years
Until the day came
When childhood changed
And we adults forgot how to play

Be young, be innocent
Be pure, be holy
Be young, be innocent
Be pure, be holy

I used to go to parties
I used to stay out late to play
I used to dance way past midnight
And work ten hours a day

Until the day came
When I heard the call
To go back to school
It was just what I needed
To renew my life
And show me some possibilities

Be young, be innocent
Be pure, be holy
Be young, be innocent
Be pure, be holy

You can have a practice
You can have a trade
You can have a study
And still have time to play
Share your gifts with children
And help them find the way

Let peace be shared
Throughout the land
And kindness kisses
The wedding band

Be young, be innocent
Be pure, be holy
Be young, be innocent
Be pure, be holy

Each Moment, I Cherish, Emmanuel

By William Bertrand

Each moment, I cherish, Emmanuel
Each friendship with you
There is, Scarlet, in my rainbow
There is no violet blue
Shall we grow old together
Without a child or two?
Each moment, I cherish, Emmanuel
Each friendship with you

Love is so mysterious
We smile with each hello we say
But see us run and hide
When we make a small mistake
You show yourself my love
In kindness and gentle words
When we adopt a friend
You adopt both of us as well

Deep within the darkness
In the recess of our soul
Reside the gifts of love
Which are still unknown
The different forms of love
In the vast diversity
Brings each of us together
In our humanity

We can see life with the sun setting
Or see life with the sun rise
It all depends on where you are, where you are
Love is not too far
But when we look with eyes of children
And love each person we meet
We shall surely have bodies like rainbows
When together, in Heaven, we meet

Concluding Remarks

I am glad that the sun
Walks with me all of the time
The water comes to me at my feet
When I walk in the ocean
Why would I wonder what God can always do
For me and you?
Signs of God bless me in many ways
How great things have happened in fifty-five years
I know the Lord is with you and me
See what God can do for you
The moon shines bright in my window
And the sun is walking with me
God is working, and I know it
Yes, we need to share experience with everyone
To read what we have discovered
In our walk with the Lord
Knowing that the Lord made the day and night
To be free from sin and fear
Keep trusting in the spirit of God work

Cynthia

William Bertrand and Cynthia Stork

Thank you for our time together
It is in the longing to belong
That we experience the desert
And the beauty of the wild flowers
When the gentle rain comes
And the savannah blooms
With the seeds of love for eternity
Let us welcome the rain
Let us welcome each other
And blossom into friends

Blessed are the People
Who maintain the home
Prepare the table and provide the food
Invite the People and serve
To create a dwelling place for Friendship
To flourish

We are blessed to be in God's
Inner and outer world
To bring people to God in a simple way
Is a blessing
Enjoy your friendship with each other!

Thank you, thank you, and thank you!

William and Cynthia

Group Discussion Topics

Moving to a new city
1. Why did you or would you re-locate?
2. What were/are your expectations?

Being a stranger
1. How does it feel to be on the "Outside"?
2. How have knocking on doors, seeking opportunities, and asking for help been working out for you?
3. What do you have to offer in relationships?

"Digging your well"- connecting to supports
1. What kind of supports do you need?
2. How do you connect to your supports?

Forging new paths
1. What kind of ventures have you tried to organize and implement?
2. How do you handle obstacles, rejection and failure?

Being a servant
1. Describe your process of getting established.
2. How have people helped you?
3. What are the joys and difficulties of your work?
4. How do you "recharge your batteries"?

Longing to go home
1. How do you keep in touch with your family?
2. In what ways do you cherish your family?
3. What are some of the signs to come back home?

Renewal
1. What in life do you take for granted?
2. How have your attitudes in life changed over time?
3. How do you give back to our Creator?

Exploitation
1. In what ways are you being exploited and oppressed?
2. How does it feel to not be valued?
3. What parts of your life do you need to improve?

Welcoming a stranger
1. How welcoming are you to strangers?
2. Tell a story about discovering goodness in a stranger.

Giving and receiving blessings
1. In what ways have people been a blessing to you?
2. How have you been a blessing to others?
3. Who in your life are you thankful for? Why?

Gifts
1. What are your personal gifts?
2. How do you like to share your gifts?

Diversity
1. How broad and diverse are your friendships?
2. How do you practice your faith?

Tears of Joy
1. Describe a situation when you had tears of joy when you were liberated?
2. How does it feel to be refreshed?
3. In what new ways are you moving forward?

Becoming a good friend
1. Describe the process of becoming a friend.
2. What kinds of activities do you like to participate in?
3. Why is friendship important to you?
4. Describe your home away from home and your extended family.

The makings of a great community
1. What are the features that make a great community?
2. What are the needs of your community?
3. How has your city helped you to grow?
4. In what ways can you become an inviting person?

CPSIA information can be obtained
at www.ICGtesting.com
Printed in the USA
BVHW070559160122
625952BV00001B/60